What Animals Are In The Back Yard?
By Anne Stratioti

What Animals Are In The Back Yard? By Anne Stratioti

Dedicated to my Dad for sharing the love of photography, to my Mom for sharing the love of reading, and to my niece, Gabrielle, with whom I look forward to sharing all that is in my back yard.

Copyright 2015 Anne Stratioti
Photos by Anne Stratioti and Tony Cooper
All Rights Reserved
ISBN: 1536930512
ISBN-13: 978-1536930511

My back yard is in the north woods of Wisconsin. We have lots of trees and fields and lots of animals that visit the back yard.

Some of the smallest animals in the back yard are insects. My favorites are butterflies and moths.

Butterflies and moths can be very small, or very big.

How many colorful butterflies and moths can you find in your back yard?

There are lots of different grasshoppers in the back yard. They come in many colors.

Do you have grasshoppers in your back yard?

Some grasshoppers blend in with the leaves or rocks. This grasshopper looks just like the rocks. Can you find the hidden grasshoppers in your back yard?

There are lots of interesting insects and spiders to find in the back yard. Spiders are very good to have around. How many spiders can you find in your back yard?

The bees like to come to the back yard to gather nectar from the many flowers.

Dragonflies and damselflies are so pretty during the summer and they eat lots of pesky mosquitoes.

How many kinds of insects can you find in your back yard?

We see lots of birds all year long. They come in all colors and sizes. We have a bird feeder with sunflower seeds for them to eat.

The birds make beautiful sounds when calling out to each other.

How many birds can you see and hear in your back yard?

Hummingbirds come to the back yard too. Their wings move so fast that you can hardly see them. There is a special bird feeder just for them. They like sugar water the best. Have you ever seen a hummingbird in your back yard?

Eagles are very large birds with sharp talons and beaks. They can be seen in the back yard watching for small animals.

Have you ever watched an eagle flying in the sky above your back yard?

In the early summer, nests get built for baby birds. This year, three baby robins were in this nest. They were always hungry for their mommy to bring them something good to eat. She brought bugs, worms, and little frogs.

When they got too big for the nest, the baby birds hopped out of the nest and into the yard to search for bugs to eat. Do you have any bird nests in your back yard?

The chipmunks and squirrels also like to eat the sunflower seeds from the bird feeder. We have red, black, and gray colored squirrels in the back yard.

We even have a ground squirrel that likes to hide in the gutter.
Do you have squirrels and chipmunks in your back yard?

A green and a brown tree snake were found on the patio in the back yard. They like to come eat the bugs that crawl in the cracks.

There was also a pretty salamander on the patio warming up in the sun. Snakes and salamanders are good animals to have in the back yard.

Do you have any of these animals in your back yard?

We have toads that like to hide under things where it is nice and cool in the summer. They come out of hiding at night to catch bugs for dinner. Toads and frogs make lots of croaking noises which is a nice summer sound.

These cute frogs were climbing the side of the house one evening.
Can you find toads or frogs in your back yard?

This turtle laid some eggs in the sandy hillside.
It will be so exciting when the baby turtles hatch.

Do you have a pond, lake, or stream with turtles in your back yard?

There are lots of rabbits and hares where I live. They like to eat my plants and the grass in the back yard. Do you see any rabbits in your back yard?

We don't see too many skunks or raccoons in our back yard, but we do have porcupine. They are cute, but don't pet one. The quills will stick in your skin and it will hurt when they get pulled out. Ouch!

Have you ever seen a skunk or maybe a raccoon or porcupine in your back yard?

Occasionally we look out the window at the right time see these animals – coyotes. They like to howl and yip when they are excited. Have you ever seen or heard coyotes in your back yard?

In the winter, we put corn and other food out for the animals to eat when it gets harder for them to find food. The deer and turkeys like to come each day to eat. Sometimes, when many deer come to eat, they get a little rowdy.

Do deer visit your back yard?

This turkey is very big and gobbles very loud when he is trying to get another turkey's attention. The deer and turkeys share the food in the back yard.

Have you ever seen a wild turkey in your back yard?

This black bear got his picture taken on a trail camera which takes a picture when anything walks by. He was looking for something good to eat.

Do you live in a place that has bears?

This momma bear and cubs were eating some apples and got their picture taken by a trail camera too. How many bears do you see in this picture?

Trail cameras are great for seeing what animals come in the back yard when you aren't around. Many animals such as bobcats, coyotes, and fishers avoid coming out when people are around. Do you think you have animals that you never see in your back yard?

The very best animal to find in the back yard is our dog, Bingo. He loves to watch all these other animals from the windows of our house.

What animals can you find in your back yard?